DO I NOT MATTER?

The residual you left behind

By: Vanessa Canteberry

Copyright @2017 By Vanessa Canteberry

All rights reserved. No part of this publication may be reproduced, stored in a retrieval system, or transmitted in any form or by any means electronic, mechanical, photocopying, recording, or otherwise without written permission of the author.
Limits of Liability-Disclaimer

The author and publisher shall not be liable for your misuse of this material. The purpose of this book is to educate and empower. The author and/or publisher do not guarantee that anyone following these techniques, suggestions, tips, ideas, and/or strategies will become successful.

The author and/or publisher shall have neither liability nor responsibility to anyone with respect to any loss or damage caused, or alleged to be caused directly or indirectly by the information contained in this book.

TABLE OF CONTENT

Foreword 1

Dedication 3

Introduction 5

Chapter 1: Where's Your Village? 6

Chapter 2: The Unknown 13

Chapter 3: The Product of a Broken Parent 20

Chapter 4: Mending Fences 28

Chapter 5: You Left Me 36

Chapter 6: Harsh Reality 45

Chapter 7: The Bleeding Heart 51

Acknowledgments 57

About the Author 59

FOREWORD

By
Dr. Aikyna Finch
www.aikynafinch.com

What we do and how we ask, as parents and adults, shapes the lives of the children around us who are watching. It affects their interactions with others for years to come. We, as adults, need to take responsibility for the impact that we had on these young lives and make it right. Regardless of the situation at the time, these children deserve to start their lives baggage-free. As a life coach, I meet with people who are not meeting their fullest potential because of a limiting belief that was placed on them as children. They have carried this belief with them for so long they believe it is legal when it usually is not the case. Children value our opinions and advice, whether they act like it or not. We are the role model, and when we steal their choices because of the decisions we make, we need to make it right.

As a child, my mother made decisions that affected my life because of the decisions that her mother made to affect her life. She was determined not to give me the foundation that she was given in life. Her mother lived the life she wanted, in spite of her children's existence, whereas my mother lived her life because of my existence. So, because my mother had no attention or focus on her, I had all the attention and focus on me. Because of this behavior during my upbringing that carried into adulthood, my mother still suffers from feelings of not being loved, depression, self-doubt, etc. In spite of the attention I received, I also received all of the things my mother suffered from as well because it was always in the atmosphere. She did a good job, and I was successful, but I still ended feeling the things she tried so hard to keep me from feeling.

My mother never got that 'make it right' moment from her mother because she believed it was over, and my mother needed to let it go. But my mother never let it go and is still carrying it to this day. Do not do this to the children that are around you. Do not let them carry baggage that has nothing to do with them. Let the burdens end with you and teach the children how not to start new baggage in their lives and for their children to come. In this book, Vanessa will tell her story and then give you strategies about how to protect and nurture our greatest assets - Our children. Take and use these strategies so you can break the cycle and give your children the baggage free life that they deserve!

DEDICATION

Often when raised in a single-parent household, the children are caught in the crossfire of the parents. Unknown emotional and psychological damage can transpire in their childhood and show up in their adult life due to the effects of feeling as if they do not matter. But ... they do matter!

Our children are screaming out but are we listening?

Parents, we need to show up and remember the purpose that was given to us at birth. Therefore, we need to show our children they have a purpose to know they do matter in this world.

INTRODUCTION

It becomes an epidemic when there are more children being raised in a single-parent household. It's also common when it should not be stereotyped, especially by race and/or the community we live in. Unfortunately, it happens every day, and more of our children are getting away from their core value which needs to be constantly instilled in them daily.

Having been raised in a single-parent household, and now raising my children as a single parent and surrounded by single parents who have something in common with me raising our children as single parents this is a huge problem, which affects our children. It's bigger than us and needs to be addressed in the way of seeking some resolution.

We have a gem in our presence, but for some reason, they feel as if they were coal, coal that is consistently overlooked and feeling misplaced but in reality, they are diamonds in the making that need to be polished off in order to shine.

Join me is shining up our diamonds of the next generation to understand that they Do Matter.

WHERE'S YOUR VILLAGE?

There was a time when the village included the Madeas, neighbors, friends, family, and even friends of the family in watching, protecting, and guiding our children. There were affordable afterschool programs not to leave any child behind. There were teachers who cared and took pride in taking care of our children who spent the majority of their time with them. The parents were involved in every aspect of making sure the homework, chores were completed before their children could even go out with their friends. The parents knew one another and kept a close look out for the children in the neighborhood, double-checking to make sure they did their homework, chores as well and reminding them to stay out of trouble. They all came together as a team to ensure the children were on the right path, no matter what.

When there was parent-teacher conference or any event taking place at the school, somebody was always present to support, even when the parents were unable to attend. The parents were fully informed by the village of friends of the updates, as if they were present, to still show love and support to their children. Knowing you have the support to keep you going is what our children need, and back in the days, they had it. Even when a parent was called to come up to the school for an emergency meeting, there was always somebody on standby to step in when the parent was unavailable.

We need to get back to creating a thriving support system to stand in the gap so our children don't fall short. Not only the children but also, as parents, we need genuine loved ones around us to vent our frustration or a shoulder to lean on. We have more in common than we are willing to accept and can do more together than we do apart as parents. Parents also need to have an escape plan to know they are not in it alone. To have an outlet to vent their frustration to at least agree and/or not agree while the respect still stayed intact. Having a parent support system to vent out when you need a shoulder to lean on or gain sound advice without judgment.

Although our children matter, we, as parents, matter as well. We need to uplift one another on all levels; we need one another to share a moment and have grown-up conversations, to live a little, or even take the load off and watch the children for a couple of hours. At times, we need each other's prayers, guidance, support, and/or even financial assistance.

It was a point in time when there would be neighborhood block parties. The neighbors would come together a couple of times a year and have celebrations. Celebrating life, birthdays; forming friendships, fundraisers, and even collaborating to make a difference, not only in the community but involving the children. Backyards barbeque to start off the summer, preparing for summer camp, stressing the importance of education and having them read books while they were out of school.

The village no longer exists. It seemed as if the older the children become, the less available the parent was. The less available the parent was, the more the children strayed and ended up in questionable situations. The more uncomfortable the circumstances became, the smaller the village appeared. We need to bring back the village to help us guide the next generation with the importance of wisdom, integrity, and education.

Children appreciate the little things in life. As kids, they need to focus on enjoying life and not bother themselves with adult decisions (e.g., deciding on which parent to side with when the adults cannot find a way to get along). Allow the child to appreciate the small things in life, such as having a hot meal to eat, clean clothes to wear, a stable home to reside in not the confusion of losing their innocence in our lost souls of being adults who seem unable to pull it together.

Being raised by a single parent provided the opportunity to attend summer camp and experience adventures I probably would have never experienced. Especially, being raised in a poverty-stricken area. At the same time, being a kid, I didn't have a care in the world playing ball, jump rope competitions, and attending birthday parties.

I had the chance to take my wandering mind off thinking about how some of my peers would spend the summer with their other parent while I was spending time, bonding with strangers trying to see where I would fit in. It was a feeling I was unable to explain due to the knowledge that my feelings did not matter, regardless of my unanswered questions of hoping I would be included in the bonding process with both parents and not just one.

I understood the feeling, as I could see the concerns within my own children's eyes. Being unable to fully articulate their feelings, all I could do was hug them tighter. I found myself falling short to lashing out my frustration the same way it was lashed out when my parents could never agree to disagree.

At times, I truly did not recognize the pattern until I had to step back from the surrounding I was accustomed to. Once I finally realized the damage I was carrying, I could only imagine the part I played in possibly damaging my children as well. As parents, we will never know it all, but at some point, we have to do better and grab a village of people who are willing to call us out on the things we fail to accept and/or may not even recognize.

Between the schools and government, significant changes have taken place. A change leaves the parents feeling hopeless and afraid to ask for help. The treatment given as if you were not responsible and/or uneducated to climb out of the low-income bracket and crime infested neighborhood.

Too often we, as single parents, are prejudged without a fair chance of getting to know the amazing person who is going through a hardship and doesn't need the extra judgment placed on them. Still, in all, we get up and work hard to provide for our children. We are taxpayers and voters who are treated like second-class citizens, and this shouldn't be.

DO I NOT MATTER?

The system is setup with parameters for us to be limited as to what we should do when disciplining our children and to the point where the household is controlled to fail. Failing to the point that if there is a discipline of the children, the courts step in, and now, not only are our children in the system, but we are labeled as a bad parent. Who is really getting any resolution from this situation? Not the children. The children are back to running away from their parent, household and running rapidly wherever they go. But again, if something happens to the child, it falls back on the parent. There is a time and a place for the courts to be involved.

Another example is, allowing the parents to remain comfortable in receiving assistance from the government (i.e., food supplements, housing, etc.) without making efforts of improving to upgrade from this temporary solution. There need to be guidelines in place to be followed across the board, regardless of your race or nationality.

There needs to be an improvement in the jobs in which employees are paid just enough to survive as well as those in which employees are living below the poverty level. It's a problem when it can cost up to $60,000 a year to keep an inmate, and the majority of households don't earn that amount a year. That can earn a student a better college education for more than one year.

I started working part time when I was in 7th grade. I used to work for a program that I was involved in, which catered for people in poverty-stricken areas and provided them the tools of knowing there is a better way. No judgment of any sort was allowed. I learned so much in this program that I was contracted until I graduated elementary school. At the same time, you can only continue the assignments if your grades were on target and if you needed a tutor, one was provided. If you excelled in your academics, you were rewarded to attend special outings. If there were issues at home, there was someone to assist. At the same time, it taught me that teamwork, communication skills, dedication, and hard work pay off. We need to bring these types of programs back into this generation.

We are quick to blame others for our issues today, but we don't support one another. We fight each other for every little issue and now, there exists a bigger issue that could've been prevented. At the same time, we need to come together to know we have more in common together plus, we can make a difference together if we remove our issues as if we were the only ones going through it.

Now, do you understand why it's important we need the village? There is more than enough statistics for us to fail as a single-parent household. However, we need to run it as if we had a village supporting our household. Become a part of a dominant team involved in raising the next generation. You can create your tribe of the village that is willing to stand on the battlefield for our children to not be left behind and in all, understand we are doing it for them. They matter, no matter what society portrays of their version of a single parent.

The more we allow the system to make changes and we don't speak up or better yet, protect ourselves we will continue to have a poverty mindset, unable to make adjustments to change our situation to protect not ourselves but our children's future.

It's vital we come together in one accord and make sure we leave our unresolved 'between-parents' issues at a distance and focus on being great role models to our children. Our children will be the ones we would appreciate taking care of us in our seasoned years. Therefore, let us avail ourselves the opportunity to be the prime example of raising the next generation better than our parents', rather than the systems determining our worth.

We are in the land of opportunity; seize the moment!

THE UNKNOWN

Relationships. They are developed gradually from being an acquaintance. Too often we tend to move hastily as if we were going to miss out of a special bond of getting to know a person, only to end up full-speed ahead and now playing house from living together, through splitting the cost of the household responsibilities, to missing out the opportunity of establishing goals too. We are cooking, cleaning, and serving it up on a platter but not fully committed due to never having an adult conversation.

We go through everyday life without truly experiencing if the person with whom we are in a relationship will be able to handle hardship. There will be hardship; you probably haven't dealt with it yet because the relationship skipped over vital moving parts and went straight to the honeymoon stages without the wedding ceremony.

Being raised in a single-parent home provided us the vision of what can transpire in the raising of our children if we tend to take note. The relationship between a mother and son is a bond in which you are teaching him where love comes from, as being the mother to love him first. The mother who took care of him when he was sick and nursed him back to health. The mom who soothed his fall and told him everything would be okay. The mom who holds him when he experiences his first heartbreak. You are providing him the blueprint on how to take care of his future wife and daughter when it's time for him to settle down.

Raising a son shows him the emotional side of a woman as well. Having been abandoned and experiencing heartbreak, a single mom can't seem to explain things to her children verbally. However, the children are watching and taking notes; they see their mother cry due to the pain from the one she loves, but they can't seem to understand the message that is being delivered or where this constant pain stems from.

Knowing the pain of a woman, as we are emotional, if we do not clearly set a distinction between being a parent and letting them go to grow, we can and will enable them permitting them to use women until they get what they want. With time, it becomes a constant habit, and now he's so far gone because you enabled him way too long. Enabling your child this way rather makes you a part of the problem than being the solution to letting them grow on their own.

Recalling my first relationship but not truly understanding the experience of building a friendship caused unnecessary heartache. Being so young and not having a consistent father figure did not make it any better. I was unsure of what to look for or questions to ask and still trying to understand what I wanted in a friendship, let alone a relationship.

These are the moments that a parent prepares their child for them not to walk around lost and confused. We, as parents, need to set a better example so our children don't become an example of the devastating pain they see us experience.

We have to cut the umbilical cord and allow them to make decisions for themselves at a reasonable age. Therefore, we have more than enough time to mold them to be respectful children, to understand they would not want anyone to harm the most important woman in their life, and it's not okay to harm another woman.

Manhood comes along with protection. Protect every being of the woman to know you have her best interest. At the same time, women have to stop giving men the benefit of the doubt when they have shown flat out disrespect. We cannot continue to give them a pass to keep doing it again. Yes, we all will make mistakes, but it is no longer considered a mistake if you continue to do the same thing over again.

What happens when the pain is gone for the moment, and everything goes back to normal? Well, at least that is the prescription that is given to return to the same place that caused you pain. The laughter is echoing throughout the house, and the smiles have yet to leave your cheeks. Still, in all, there is a pain that's been buried yet again and holds a trademark in your heart. You are trying to prove a point, but to whom? You, your children, your friends, or the person who continues to disappoint you time and time again? But you continue to take this person back every time, hoping they change. When in a relationship, you have to determine your position and if you see yourself as part of the team. Or are you just an object hoping to get your chance to be considered to becoming a power couple for an important role?

DO I NOT MATTER?

As we are still trying to have a life, we have to keep in mind the life example we are creating for the next generation to repeat. We have to be honest with ourselves as if we could see ourselves in their eyes. Do we want them to experience this type of relationship in their adult life? Your son will treat a woman with the utmost respect if you teach and show him the importance of a woman and how valuable she is in his life.

Unfortunately, when there is a bad breakup between parents, the children are lost in the shuffle. They are being shuffled from home to home and having to hear their parents complain, but at the same time, not understanding why their parent moved onto loving someone else. The breakdown in the communication shows up when the children become adults attempting to live their lives. They experience the breakup as well from abandonment, through blaming themselves, to trying to find their position in the relationship of a broken home.

This is why it is so essential to own our truth. Take, for example, a woman who has daddy-daughter issues that were not resolved, and now she is dating. She is dating and also consistent in looking at every man to replace the position of her father. Why? Because those issues were not addressed. It's likely her dad had issues of his own and had no clue how to fix himself and never accepted the fact that his own mother did not teach him the value of love due to her having her own daddy issues. Now we have a pattern going, and our sons will not allow anyone to get too close because they had a bad experience with how their mom treated them;

therefore, the wall goes up, and the woman that really cares can't get through because of his issues he has yet to address.

Often when a woman has a pattern of dating men after a breakup, it starts from the man she was supposed to look up to and love first—he left her to figure out how to receive genuine love from someone else. She's seeking a void to be filled but looking for love in the wrong man. You attract who you are, and now you are dating a split image of the father due to the representation of himself he gave to you.

I always wonder what it would be like to be a daddy's girl. Would he take me to the park, push on the swings, or even chase me around until I tapped out? Maybe taking his little girl on an adventure just to see the world in her eyes. Introducing the guy who sparked my interest, pursued me as a man should; the man that I learned to love first—my father.

However, I never had the opportunity to experience this type of relationship due to issues my parents still had long after me. The constant interference from both sides left me feeling as if I did not matter enough to have them put their issues to the side. The bond you prayed for melted before getting the experience; the glue which was sufficient to mend us together dried away.

I found myself asking the same questions when I was in a complicated situation with my children's father. It's hard to see that I allowed myself to place my children in a vicious cycle which I had already experienced. I had to grow up and bit my tongue more, do things just to keep the peace as much as possible. It was not easy, but I eventually learned, little by little, how to cope with co-parenting, even when it seems as if I were still playing both roles. Again, I had to own up to the position I placed myself in and take responsibility and do better.

When you don't take the time to get to know and understand your past, you will accept other people's past as your own, and unfortunately, you have accepted the dysfunction to continue questioning yourself, Do I not matter? We have to end the silent pain we felt as children, but now, looking at our lives as an adult, we wonder, How did we stay here in pain for so long? We stayed because nobody wanted to address and/or accept the answers that came from the mystery box of questions.

No longer did I want to feel a void of questions I knew nobody wanted to answer. At the same time, I had to be honest with myself: Did I really want to know the answer, and would it be the truth? Sometimes, we have to accept people who don't want to accept their truth but would rather point their finger at the next person to avoid the truth.

Even in my adult life with children, questions never became apparent as to how they got to the place of ignoring the fact that who caused the pain continually reappeared. The finger pointing game was getting old, and decisions had to be made for me to move on. I had to make the decision for my sanity so I can move on and discover I do have an opportunity to get it right with my children.

While my children were sleeping, I would pray for them to keep their minds out of confusion—to give me clarity to be honest and open enough with them to answer questions that I didn't want to answer but needed to answer, as I know what it feels like to seek out answers to the questions and still end up empty. I did not want them to feel empty. Again, I had to own my position as being an adult and a parent to my children and make sound decisions going forward at the same time, preparing myself to answer questions they may have, to be open and honest without overlooking their feelings.

We have to keep in mind to include the feelings of the children, no matter what. We may feel they may not be watchful or understand the distance between two parents, but they do. Regardless of how frustrated my children may feel as a result of the reaction of their parents, I would always tell them, "You may not like it, but you have to respect your parent."

Never leave a signed letter ending with 'Unknown'!

THE PRODUCT OF A BROKEN PARENT

Too often relationships are formed, and history is not discovered until after the fact. Patterns are overlooked, and fingers begin to point. The results, unfortunately, become a child that's left behind due to a broken relationship. With too much ego at stake, the children fall in between the parents.

At what point will this vicious cycle end? When will we give our children a fair chance to make it out and not discover our mess? It's not one-sided; it's both. Too much hatred shows up in our parenting, and when relationships end, we tend not to fight harder to become better co-parents since we couldn't get it right as a couple. Our children not only deserve both parents, but they need to see the respect for one another come together (for the sole purpose of the child); they don't have to go yet unnoticed due to us failing them.

Sometimes staying in the home can make it seem as if there were a body holding wasted space to confuse the children into believing it's okay. No parent-and-child relationship, and there's only a response from the parent when the child is disobedient. There needs to be an all-around parent, regardless of what issues you may be experiencing. The home is so broken the parents stop mending it, as it was too far off investing in any more time to nurture the relationship that died a long time ago. Again, is it worth to stay in a home to be a representation of a stable family structure for the sake of the children?

There are many parents who are experiencing turmoil in the home but determine to stay together to prove a point to the children and/or outsiders looking in. At the same time, behind closed doors, you are miserable, and so are the children, even though they haven't expressed it. However, they are taking notes, and this is the memory you have set up for them, as to what to expect when it's time for them to be in a toxic environment and/or relationship. You have taught them to stay and stick it out for the sake of the children, and you all suffer in silence. This is the pattern of yet another cycle you have taught them unintentionally.

Don't continue to paint a picture that states, "It's okay to stay in a place that is unrepairable." Remember, it took two to create a miracle; it will take the same two to come together to make an adult decision to stay or go their separate ways without involving the children to have to make a decision because we can't afford to have them caught-up in our feelings.

Celebrating our children's accomplishments such as graduations, a great report card, passing an exam you studied so hard for and passed with flying colors these little things count. Unfortunately, many children have yet to see to their parents in the same room to celebrate their success. My parents were so caught up in their own emotions; only one parent attend my graduation. Did the other parent know the details prior to? I don't believe so, but still, in all, I blamed myself for many years and asked, Do I not matter?"

Even when the parents moved on to be in another relationship and left behind their current children, again, Do I not matter? keeps replaying over and over in a child's mind. It hurts the child to know you moved on and now the contact is barely recognizable due to you focusing on your newfound love—when your first love should always be your children, no matter what.

Things may not work out between the both parents; always keep your mind in direct connection with doing right in the sight of your children. Even if you fill the other parent is wrong, do your part, and eventually, the child will come to their conclusion when the time is right. They may not say much, but trust me, they are noting the behavior we express.

Physical, mental, verbal, and emotional abuse exist, and it can become the determinant of your every being if you continue to stay in a broken environment. often when a parent comes from a broken home, they usually experience some type of abuse, and if they haven't rectified the issue, it becomes a traceable habit from being in relationships, through being a parent to avoid the feelings as if you didn't matter to replacing it with somebody to make you feel as if you mattered.

Even though both of my parents came from a two-parent household, they both experienced brokenness from their upbringing, which manifested in their adult lives. We have to be willing to understand the starting point that caused us to become broken parents. Then how can we move forward in healing from a place of acceptance to forgiveness, and then the transformation to move forward not to allow our children to be in the position of relating to something that we, as parents, should have confronted ahead of time?

It takes more than money to raise our children, praying for them, instilling wisdom in them, teaching them the importance of having integrity and being a person of character. Showing up and being present means the world to them. You're giving them hope for a better outcome of a single-parent home. Your time to attend a parent-teacher conference or after-school activities will show them you truly care about their future. Pick up the phone just because of them; be a listening ear to allow them to be heard.

Quality time to share some secrets or to laugh at corny jokes can make their day seem alright. Advise them on how to handle situations with a better outlook on life. Teach them how we went wrong so they can make better decisions than we did.

The society gives us a dirty look as being a single parent who could not get it right. We are placed in a category we all don't belong. We need to come together to give the society something to talk about, as some amazing parents have stepped up to the plate and raised some amazing children to become a better person than what the society thought of them. Give them something to talk about!

Coming from broken parents creates an etch-a-sketch, vivid picture of our future. Never understanding broken places is what would become of you if you decide to follow the stretches you envisioned in your childhood. Children have a vivid imagination they are not afraid to dream big and love to go on an adventure of the unknown.

I come from two parents who had both parents in the home, but in reality, it seemed as if no one was home both parents going in the opposite directions and were not on the same page but determined to stay in the household until the children are old enough to live on their own. Time wasted that we cannot get back.

Staying in the home can bring on confusion, and leaving can do the same. Whatever, the decision may be, always keep the child as the priority. Having an open and honest conversation as adults and being on the same page is huge not leaving the other parent to explain to the child why the other parent is playing disappearing acts. We have to keep the children normal, functioning, living with the most important role models in their lives.

Once there is a breakup, the adults are too focused on their emotional baggage and carry bitterness, as now their life is turned upside down, but what about the child? Many days, I wonder if my parents would ever come together to be able to have a normal conversation or not talk down the other parent or better yet, not allowing the parent to see the child, and now using them as a pawn. Our children need as much stability as possible, and consistency is key.

Raising my children, I had learned a lot, especially being a teen mom. I never knew there was such a love that depends on you for everything. Trying to hold it together to make their life better than mine. Going without, so they can have. Losing sleep to find a better way to resolve ongoing issues. Finding ways to heal my dying soul, hoping it will heal in enough time to not be damaged beyond repair.

Parents, we have to stop walking away when we feel it's too hard to deal with the parent of our children. We don't have the leisure of walking away because we played a role in creating the next generation. We have to own our part and, by any means, refuse to break our children because we are broken. Our children need us; therefore, you have to know you are needed for your child to understand the role they will possibly be involved in when the time comes.

After realizing the broken place my parents came from, I had to accept it. Regardless, if you agree to it or not, life can beat you up, but when you have not experienced life, and you get thrown into a place of the unknown, you will have more challenges.

We can't hold the children at fault due to the decision of their parent. Plenty of times, I seen parents leave the child to be sent off to the wolves way too soon having issues that they refuse to face, but now the child is taking the place of the person who let them down. All the aggression is spoken into the children mentally, destroying every cell in their body. It's like giving them oxygen with no mask to suppress your pain, but they are slowing suffocating.

Being present gives them hope of the possibilities for tomorrow. There's not a price you can pay to replace the value of our children. Your time is measured by creating unforgettable memories which can be replayed like a broken record over again in our minds, but it is priceless on the inside.

Your children need you to instill and build their confidence, character, and substance for life lessons. You are needed in more ways than you may never know. Your existence gives them a touch that makes them feel as if they could conquer the world by the value you instilled in them. It's like they finished the race, regardless of how bad their muscle hurt from all the training and how exhausted they felt due to the lack of sleep. However, seeing their parent motivated them on to finish the impossible race they knew they would not have won; seeing you was worth the perseverance to receive the most valuable award of the year. They are happy knowing that you, their parent, are waiting with arms outstretched to be the first to say the words they long to hear: "I am so proud of you"; "You make me a better person because of you"; "I love you."

There would be times I would drop my children off to see their father, and I would wait outside so they can have their moment only. Even if it was for five minutes, it was memorable. I was learning growth as a mother and knowing what it felt like looking for a father in place of my father who was not consistent. We tend to leave out the pain, instead of addressing it, because we feel running is better than facing it. I had to face it to accept it.

I remember in my adult life asking the same questions, Do I not matter? as I had seen my parents argue over old issues that were still a hot topic on their minds, and both have moved on to not move on. I no longer wanted to be in their presence, as they were still focusing on who was right and who was wrong, and ignoring the fact that my siblings and I were still caught in the crossfire of the swords of tongues as they exchanged words.

I needed my parents, but in reality, my parents needed to find themselves in their struggle of not willing to accept the unknown of their truth. Until you accept your truth, your future exists on false pretenses. To be open to embracing your future, you must face your truth, even if you may not like the needle that stings your back in the process of accepting the pain of your past.

Our children need parents, not a parent to be our friend.

MENDING FENCES

When you are determined to be right and get stuck in your ways, you build a wall of unresolved issues of unresolved mysteries. The more you ignore them, the more time you are losing in finding why you remain guarded, thus allowing the wall to be your source of protection.

I had to accept that I, too, had created a wall to keep out people who had a pattern of hurting me in some ways. I no longer wanted to give them the permission to destroy my inner peace.

At times, the road map may appear as if it were leading you off the destination (your goal). You have to envision the map as guiding you to make a decision to stay on the road in order to reach your ultimate goal. The ultimate goal of accepting the things you cannot change and working hard to grow and learning to do things differently than the box placed in front of you. The box is a representation of dumping your baggage and leaving it there to be shipped to the dumpster. You do not belong inside the box; do not allow others to label you as someone who repeats bad habits they were taught.

DO I NOT MATTER?

Those who broke you cannot fix you. You have to be willing to accept that they are broken, too, and need to do the working in fixing themselves. If they choose to work on them, there's a possibility of mending the fence.

We need not adjust ourselves to receive love from our parents. But at the same time, we need to understand it's a bigger life example that was on display. They are living with the guilt of not being able to give you the best life. They have to live with you while remaining in your feelings, with the possibilities of them repeating the same cycle to their children.

Ask yourself: Is it worth holding on to the past because you feel you are owed an explanation and/or an apology? It will be a hard pill to swallow, but you need to accept those things you are not able to change; you need to be willing to make the change for the better.

I had to come to terms with allowing individuals who I no longer give access to control my feelings. I refused to carry on my thoughts of questions, which I learned to bury away to accept the part in which I played a role.

Growing up in a single-parent household, you will hear all types of excuses as to why the other parent is not involved in the child's life, why things didn't work out between the parents. Whatever the case may be, the child is here and still needs to be raised in a positive environment with a team of role models who are ready and step up.

However, too often when a relationship ends, and especially if it's on wrong terms, the agreement amongst

DO I NOT MATTER?

adults is transferred and terminated to include the child. No, it's not fair, but it happens too often.

I remember there would be times when my parents disagreed, and the other parent would keep their distance in order to keep the peace. In reality, how is this resolving the issue when the children need their parents? There would be times when we would wait for my father to show up for a planned visit, even until now but he never called or showed up. This has become a pattern, especially for me because, usually, I never went on visits with my brothers to see my father. I would stay at home with my mom. Why? Good question. I stopped asking and started to watch more of my parents' reactions.

When I had the courage enough to confront my unresolved issues with my parents, it was a blame game as to why things turned out the way they did. Never taking ownership of the role they played, which caused me to feel as if it were my fault or that I did not matter.

Once I came to terms with not understanding the direction of their decisions, I had to let it go in order to move on. It's interesting how things you learned to ignore can reappear in your life unexpectedly.

After becoming a teen mother, I wanted to give my children all the love and attention their hearts desired. In reality, as they grow up, they will ask questions, and they will turn to their parents, seeking answers. When the time came for me to answer the questions, being a single mother, I had to go back and get answers from my own parents.

DO I NOT MATTER?

It's interesting how life can repeat itself and immaculate your life in ways that are unexplainable. I had to get peace with not having answers for my children and find a better way to co-parent without the drama. This role as being a parent is so hard, and it's unrelatable when you don't have children to give sound advice.

Have you ever felt a hurt so bad you started to blame yourself? You are now questioning every person that attempts to befriend you, as you never knew their intentions, but at the same time, not giving them the benefit of the doubt? Well, that was me. I've been hurt so much; I was damaged. Damaged enough to damage the next person that was getting too close. My words were so harsh, and it radiated off me to the point people knew not to approach me with the look I carried upon my face.

I carried the pain, the world, my children, the endless unresolved issues, and missing being a child all at the same time. I was an adult trapped in a child's body screaming to come out and play with dolls once again. I wanted to crawl into my parent's bed so they would stroke my head while I cried myself to sleep, but I knew it was all a dream. Still, in all, I have to be parents to my children.

I wanted to gain their respect of my children, knowing that I have their best interest. Love them hard enough to know they have a place locked solidly in my heart, understanding that I am cheering them onto being better than I could ever be at their age.

I had to be a student while parenting my children so I could get some things right while I had the time.

DO I NOT MATTER?

Regardless of the role my parents played or their parents', I need to be able to get it right because I didn't have the best village. I had to mend the fences with my parents with all the questions and mysteries which left me asking myself, Do I matter? I never wanted to continue down the path of having my children to feel the way I felt for years.

I had to be an adult and have a conversation with my parents, separately, to find a better way of resolving issues that nobody wanted to address. I lay at night with my thoughts and questions, seeking answers. The majority was ignored, and then there's the finger-pointing game from one parent to another.

My ultimate goal was to wipe the slate clean because I needed my parents to be better grandparents to my children. Needless to say, it was temporarily resolved, and I accepted the outcome of moving and taking back my power of inner peace, knowing I put myself out to get answers, of which majority was not answered. Sometimes the answers are not in the conversation; it's in the body language.

As adults, sometimes we get so caught up in our stuff, and we end up losing precious gems along the way. I was willing to do the work on myself so I can enjoy the gems of knowledge and people that appreciate me as a person. Gems are meant to be soaked up to admire the jewel within. You are a jewel; keep picking up the gems along the way in your journey of discovering who you can become.

Walking away in order for me to mend what was left of me was the hardest thing I had to face in the moment of me still trying to find my true self-worth. Even when my name was dragged through the mud, I had to do what was best for me in order to save my children from feeling the emptiness that I was experiencing in my adult life.

The emptiness I carried left me with no feeling to express the emotions I carried. Not sure how much longer I could continue this journey due to being terrified of becoming what I was accustomed to. I knew there was more; at the same time, I needed clarity to understand this magnitude of emptiness so I could become whole enough to become a better example to those who depended on me.

Gaining clarity is what I needed, and since I could not get the clarity from my parents, I had to get clear on what I would like to see the future hold for me. I was so lost and needed to be found, but I needed to accept the clarity of others not being clear with themselves; nonetheless, I was determined to be clear within the person I needed to get to appreciate. I found me.

I no longer allowed people who were determined to remain a liability on my growth, my space, let alone my strength to hold me back. I only accepted people who could be an asset in my life those who could constantly add value to my journey. In mending fences for my well-being, even for those who don't agree, they must understand the importance of it.

I no longer want to hold over my parents' heads of unresolved issues by ignoring them. I took a bold stand to address the issues and had to be okay with the outcome. Even though I understood what I was up against, I had to use wisdom to heal what was holding me hostage. You have to be honest with yourself and ask the little child in you, "How much longer can you go on with rejection?"

Parenting will never be perfect, but I learned I needed to apologize for the mistakes I made and the mess I discovered in my healing process. It did not make me less of a parent; rather, it made me a parent, being human and open enough to admit my wrongdoing.

You can truly never understand the parent's insight until you are a parent. I don't think my parents did not love their children, they were unable to show it on a continuous basis due to all the life issues they were juggling. They juggled so much they lost focus somewhere due to the challenges they struggle with on a daily basis. Sometimes, parents will never lay everything out and provide an explanation to why things turned out the way they did and due to them feeling as if they failed you somewhere. Not only you but themselves. Recognizing they can not go back and get the time lost they wasted due to their own fault. It does not have anything to do with you but at the same time, it does involve you as you are watching them unfold right in front of you.

In that very moment, I truly understood the life of a parent and what can possibly happen when you don't make better decisions to avoid anyone from being harm, who are involved in the upbringing of the children.

I wanted to ensure I was able to share my thoughts with my children, as they need to hear it from me, and not a sob story from anybody else. To move forward, I had to swallow my pride and pick up my soul ties in order to mend where I went wrong.

It made me better overall, to be vulnerable to understand I no longer had the strength to carry their pain, regardless how much I expected from them. This is the way our children will continue to feel misplaced due to us not letting things go in order for us to mend what is missing.

When I come in contact with people who I grew up with or even my children's friends, and they are seeking advice, I share my truth in hopes to help them in mending their fences. You cannot go around the fence or even through it to bypass wisdom—wisdom enough to know you can stop self-sabotaging your self-worth due to the prescription that was described.

It will not be easy, but it will take off the load you have carried for all the years. You never want to be at a point in your life where you are unloading everything on someone you cherish due to you allowing it to build up. Start making random stops to dump the loads you carry along your journey. You will be glad you did. Plus, you will be able to have a better outcome with your own family because you did the work on you and not point the fingers at others. Always keep in mind, it's better to mend in order to become a better example to those who look up to you. Give yourself permission to unload dead weight.

Let us not damage our children because somebody damaged us.

YOU LEFT ME

As parents, we do not want our children to go through life feeling as if we left them for selfish gain or to destroy them along the way. Sometimes I wonder, If parents had a better relationship of understanding what's important, would they lose focus on instilling core values into the children?

There were plenty of times my siblings would have the consistent experience of being in the presence of both parents on separate occasions. My mom would have us during the week, and my brothers would be picked up on weekends. Even though we have the same parents, it seemed as if I had a different father, and that was not the case. When my father did include me, it felt distant. There was no consistency with the bonding experience.

I felt abandoned and alone. Asking myself, What did I do wrong? Growing up, I heard various stories, but nothing was adding up. All I wanted was to be in the presence of parents that showered their children with love and creating memories.

It came to a point in my life where I was left so often; I started to grasp the concept. It was tough when you feel you are walking the streets alone to come to a dead end time and time again. Hoping to get to a destination, and somebody would take you in and see that you have a substance of value. I walked so much; I held my head down, following the cracks until it came to a stop light. The cracks were more important that I would look at them, following the path to get to my destination.

Just imagine how many more children are walking around, feeling lost and trying to find a place to fit it. It's such a lonely place, but when you are left behind, you have to find another route. Now I understand my route was rerouting me to find the map to my destiny. It took me a long time to put the pieces of the cracks together, to find my true worth, but I found it, and now it's sealed in a secure place.

At the same time, it's frustrating to see the children of today who are a split image of what I had experienced. Lost in a cold world, trying to find a position to stand on and hold tight. Again, we need the village of leaders to come together to lead the hearts of the broken, mend the fences that are ready to be bonded together and accept those things we cannot change.

When you have abandonment issues, you will attract somebody who mimics you. You will hold onto them because you have had an experience of being left by someone you loved the most who did not return the same love. When a father leaves their daughter, they take her heart with them. They take her innocence of pureness of being the princess. She needs to know she is loved by the way your treat her; the timeless piece of words. She will always cherish the way you protected her from harm's way and made sure you stressed to her brothers to always protect her while you were away. Not only are you showing her brothers how to protect her but you are teaching them how to protect women such as their mother as well. Regardless, if you are together or not, the utmost respect for the mother of your children still and always remain intact.

What happens when you make a bold decision for the both of us, but now you are away for an extended stay? You felt that being a man, your back is against the wall, but for some reason, you are now behind walls where we can no longer touch you. Too many parents end up in jail and now the children are subjected to see you behind a glass. How can you be a hands on parent? Through letters, phone calls and/or weekly visits. Have you ever asked yourself what damage will this do to the children? The mindset of the child seen you on a daily basis to now having to see you in a controlled environment with minimum interactions.

Men are given a bad representation of manhood, but in reality, too many men are raised by women. Women cannot raise our boys to be men and believe the harsh reality they can possibly face with the decisions they make. Yes, women can have an enormous impact on our men, but they do need a man's perspective as well, just like men cannot raise our daughters to be ladies. They have a great insight on teaching them how a man should treat them.

Women take their role (of being the mother who births the children) to another level when something can be resolved together. We are too busy responding to the emotional side of the issue of having to co-parent. We would rather have the authorities involved when every man or woman does not belong in the courts. In return, the issue escalates because, after all, you did not resolve your personal feeling, which did not involve the child, but you added the child, and now the parent doesn't want any parts to play for the child.

The system is designed to go against our men and agree with the woman. Unfortunately, that is not always the case. But again, the child is placed in a compromising position due to the inability of parents to resolve their issues amongst themselves.

Your personal feelings should never stop you from being involved in your children lives. How can our children make better decisions, if we as adults can not use common sense? Yes, it's understandable emotions arise when the other parent is present but again that is an issue you choose not to resolve. It's better to heal within, learn how to forgive and be the best parents to the children you can be and guide them to make better decisions.

I've seen too often the children are held as a pawn against the other parent for whatever reason. However, when the child starts to develop the ways of the other parent, they are treated different owing to the emotion that's been carried as a result of the distant parent. Is the parent really distant or is that the picture that was painted in order to make one parent placed on a pedestal of righteousness? Determining who is right or wrong, the child is still caught in the middle of immature ways.

When the other parent moved on and now is in another relationship, the parent who has yet to heal, will place limitations on the child but hold the parent accountable. Why is it we can move and be in another relationship and have the person who we are dating in the child's life but will find excuses as to why the other parent should not introduce them to the person they are now dating? It's a double standard and childish. Yes, ground rules within reason should be discussed amongst the adults. We should not have any and everybody we date introduced to our children. If it's not a serious relationship the children need not be involved. They already juggle co-parenting, that is more than enough to place our personal issues onto them as well.

Our children need to be able to have both parents in their lives, and when the time comes, they will be able to ask the questions for themselves, not due to the parents' input of mass manipulation. We have to do right by our children, no matter what; they deserve a better outcome compared to the income of information received in a venting section. Their feelings trump ours, regardless of how we feel about the other parent. Our children deserve the opportunity of seeing a prime example of parents coming together on one accord, regardless if they have moved on in other relationship. We remain a family whose ultimate goal is to love, cherish, and guide our children.

I had learned so much about me being a parent through my children's eyes. I wanted to do better to give them a reason to smile harder just to make their day but, in return, made mine as well. It was not easy, but I knew it was necessary. Their right frame of mind and outlook on better days provided me hope that I was on the right path of making a difference.

Knowing what I know now, I can understand, but unfortunately, you get to a place where you stop caring.

DO I NOT MATTER?

You stop caring because it destroys the possibilities of making a difference in your future. Even though I could not relate to a lot of things that I see now, which are important in raising the next generation, I had to accept dreaming that one day, I, too, could relate to having a bond with both parents in co-parenting.

I still remember the moment when I had to make a decision to remove myself from toxic relationships, in order to maintain my sanity. To hopefully become a better role model that my children will one day grow to appreciate.

Having to decide to walk away was harder than I imaged because I was taking my children along for a ride which I was unsure of. But at the same time, I was willing to take the risk in order to save them from me destroying them due to me holding onto my past.

How often is this still happening in this generation where children are caught in the middle of adult's issues? Parents are missing their child's point, forgetting this blessing of a child standing in their midst.

Is it that bad you cannot put your ego and pride to the side and respect the fact that the child needs and takes precedence in knowing both parents? Regardless of the issues they're still holding onto and refuse to let go, as if they were playing a game of cat and mouse, it's painful to see the reflection of anger in the child's face as they are trying to focus on their true identity, only to be constantly stuffed back into reality of the unknown due to the abandonments issues they still hold onto.

Now the child is an adult and still afraid to latch onto anything due to never wanting to experience losing them too. It's hard to explain to even someone who can relate, as you are afraid they will eventually cause you pain just like your parents did.

Too often our men find the nearest exit to escape the pressure of having to deal with life events. Especially, when they have not had a man who was consistent teaching them the core value of responsibilities. Men are taught responsibility, to be the man of the house, to watch after your mom and siblings. At some point, the young man gets a fair chance to go through the stage that leads up to the point of having to make adult decisions in a young child's mind. Men are taught to lead the household but are never willing to know the rules of manhood.

Men get a bad reputation from women as if everything fell on them just because they didn't carry the child, although they were present in creating the child. Men have feelings, and when they don't have an outlet, they tend to lash out when the pressure is squeezing their last breath. Men are taught not to show emotion, as it's a sign of weakness, when, in reality, it's a sign of being human with feelings; it's good to show the softer sign of you when needed.

When men feel they are not being heard, they check out and shut down from the world. They can be in an amazing relationship, doing well in their career but when the pressure is too much to handle, they are unsure how to express their emotions before shutting down and subject to lose everything instantly. From friends, relationship and now the children are feeling the distance. We have to stop beating them down to minimize their manhood.

DO I NOT MATTER?

There have been plenty of times I have seen the expression of emotions in men. It's something that's not shared often, but when they do show you the tender side of them, it's because they can trust you, but they won't share it with others that will do them harm.

Learning how to speak to a man in a tone for them to listen is not belittling, not screaming at the top of your lungs but in a way that is gentle. Men are more emotional than they will admit, but at the same time, do not use it to your advantage, as their guards would go up.

Also, all men don't fall into the category of running away from their responsibility; some are pushed away, and others are punished this way. Men need to understand they are needed to lead households, be involved in raising their children. Who benefits when your presence goes missing? The children!

Our men are not tools we have in our shed which we can use and put away as we please. We have to stop allowing them to feel as if they have no say in raising the children, as their opinion is just as important. Do not have them feeling the way they felt in their upbringing of being left behind.

Even adults still carry the imprint of being left behind when life is disrupted. Turbulence is constantly a battle facing the rejection of being abandoned by their parent. Women lash out in anger because it's the only way she seems to have a voice of opinion in hopes somebody will listen to her cry without stating the words and feeling verbal to have her pain taken advantage of yet once again. Once we can agree that we, too, have more in common, we can move forward in attacking what attacked us and to learn how to react in a better way so we no longer have to feel as if we didn't matter.

Save our Children; they deserve a fair chance!

HARSH REALITY

Your son is not your boyfriend; neither is he your husband. He is your son. The bond between a mother and son is something that shows the soft side of a boy who will eventually become a husband and a dad one day.

We tend to be overbearing and not willing to allow the children to live and create life lessons of their own. We cannot continue to babysit them to the point they are not willing to take up their position to produce results. Create their thoughts, decisions, and even make a mistake or two. How do you expect them to learn if you refuse to clip their wings to fly?

Raising a son, I learned what I instilled in him is showing up in his growing stages. He listens to me, even when I thought he was not listening, to understand how to respect and honor women; never to get so comfortable to disrespect her, as he comes from a woman. Plus, I also instilled in him never to allow anyone disrespect his mother or his sisters. Learning how to walk away to cool off before saying something you cannot take back or making a decision for a moment of satisfaction, only to be placed in a complicated situation of no return.

DO I NOT MATTER?

Teach your boys the importance of opening the doors, walking on the right side of the street, and even walking away to cool down in order to get your point across in a heated disagreement. I've seen many boys disrespect their mother and even the person they are dating. This happens due to the mother's enabling of her son as well as the father's disappearing acts. Again, we have to maintain a village at all times to come in from time to time to do routine checkups.

Your daughter is not your girlfriend, wife or your mom. She's not the woman you want to cater to you. Expecting her to cook, clean and/or iron your clothes. She's your daughter. You are not to disrespect her and speak to her with vulgar language in order to make your point known. She's your princess and you want to make sure you are showing her, she's your little girl. You are providing her the boundaries of not allowing a man to disrespect her on any level because you raised her with the utmost regards of respect.

Our children will challenge us but we have to remind them we are the parents and they can not put us against one another. Once they understand they can not break the parents, they will be hesitant to test the water of crossing the lines of disrespect. Why? Because we as parents came together on one accord to let it be known, we intend to raise greatness.

Women, just like you feel men play games, so do we. We will act as if we didn't know the answer and ask the question. We will question them on their whereabouts, go through their personal belongs, look for something but unsure what we'll find. Now there is an argument taking place that could have been avoided.

DO I NOT MATTER?

If you have to go through the trouble to search for answers, you need to make a decision as to whether it's worth it to stay and resolve the issues at hand. Even though things may not work out, it should never have anything to do with the child. We have to stop using the children as a crutch to make a statement. There is no need to hold the child back from attempting to have a relationship with their parent. When the time comes for questions, be honest enough, to tell the truth.

After applying the counsel of their mother, a child also knows you will always be their mom, and it is okay to allow them to explore the world of possibilities, keeping in mind the way they were raised by a single mother.

We, as parents, have hopes, dreams and would expect nothing but the best for the children. However, they would have to live with the decisions of their choice. You, as a parent, need to do your part to instill the tools of reference when the time comes.

The biggest error you, as a parent, make, whether it's your fault or not, is moving on to start a new chapter in your life but feel no need to include the children who already exist. You even took on the responsibility of somebody else's child and voided your current children. Or you have started another family but mending the family to know one another and making them feel included, regardless of what transpired in your previous relationship.

Too many of our children today are meeting their siblings and/or family members through someone else and not by the parent who should have done the introduction. It's an awkward feeling to know there is a piece of you in a world that doesn't know you but find out about you years later, and now you have mixed feelings and so much catching up to do. How do you respond when you come to find out you have another family you don't know anything about? Again, it goes back to our parents needing to make the right decision, no matter what, as you already can relate to the unknown.

It's also so heartbreaking when the child is disowned and allowed to go the direction they choose to take in the path of life. But have you taken the time to ask the child 'why'? Why do they choose the path of self-destruction? Have you ever thought they are screaming out for attention, such as your love? Yes, you are the parent, and at the same time, you are judging your child, but you have not been there to know what their life has been in time past. You, as the parent, are so quick-tempered to point the finger at everybody but unable to see that you are possibly the missing piece of the puzzle which brings the storyline together.

There were times when I made decisions that were not pleasing to my parents, and the outcome was harsh—harsh to the point where pointing fingers, pushing you off for somebody else to deal with the issue was the way to go. Still, in all, the real answers were neither discovered nor discussed. Taking on the part of being a parent, you do not decide when you are willing and ready to deal with the matters which are important to you or to avoid issues that embarrass you. Being a parent, there will be times when you will have to face situations but understand your presence and time is valuable to the children. Not your money or time.

DO I NOT MATTER?

Money is a needed to provide for the child, but you are needed in all levels of raising the children who will one day need to care for you.

Again, who is winning in this situation? Nobody! At the same time, no one wants to address the elephant in the room. We have to stop downplaying our truth. Yes, we are hurt, the relationship did not last and ended sour, but the blessing of it all is the children who are on display in front of your eyes. We have to appreciate the blessing and be willing to accept responsibility for our action and not continue to have a reaction due to us not acknowledging the result.

Too often our children are taking for a game of chess, and they never signed up for it. Moving parts into a position which should have never been touched or provoked. Now we are in a place in our lives where the extended family has no part in the child's life due to your decision. Why does the child have to be punished for our decision?

If the parent wants to be a parent in the child's life, let them. Support the decision of coming together to learn how to leave respect on the table to co-parent the children. Stop bashing one another. Put your feeling to the side and stop playing games with the children's feeling.

Our children are reacting based on our decision and response to the other parent. But this is what I've learned: overlook what needs not to be focused on. If it's not hurting your well-being or the child's, let it go. Sometimes, it's best not to entertain those who are acting as if they were from a circus looking for laughs.

DO I NOT MATTER?

This teen mom had to grow up to learn that it's better not to be a part of the problem but find a solution. I was the problem, seeking answers for the solution to resolve my issues that were not resolved; I kept reminding myself, I did not want my children to feel the same way.

It was and is still painful when some things are not in your control; you feel as if it's being controlled, but in reality, it ends up working itself out as long as you continue to do your part. I've seen much growth in myself but more smiles when I, too, can identify with my children to do all I can to do right by them.

Remember, we selected them and chose to be the parent of our children when we decided to make a grown-up decision. Our decision is and will always be to make better decisions going forward, no matter what.

Harsh is walking away, but your presence needs you to stay!

THE BLEEDING HEART

When I look at the pain in your eyes, my heart breaks. When you are searching to find a place in this cruel world, tears well up in my eyes. When I see you sitting motionless deep in your thoughts, I want to sit there and hold you tight. Then there are times I sit back and wonder, Why? Why and how did I end up in a place to make me feel lost, at the same time, questioning myself on the choices I've made which makes you feel the way you feel. Where did I go wrong? How can I stop your bleeding heart from bleeding out?

Raising children to be better than you as well as to educate them on making better decisions than you is great; however, we still have to help them to understand they are not the cause of the bleeding heart. Even though they are feeling empty inside. It's the missing piece that should have been there but, for some reason, made a decision for the both of them instead.

We have to be wise enough to use wisdom when decisions need to be made. Did we include the child? Did we take into consideration their feelings? Walking away from your children is a bold, careless decision. What about their thought process on accepting your decision and having to deal with unresolved issues in their teens and adult life?

DO I NOT MATTER?

Dealing with my parents' inability to co-parent due to someone wanting to be right and the other refusing to be wrong is not the way forward. Instead, parents should focus on making their presence known to the children. Our children learn from us, and we are teaching them how to react and respond to similar situations when they have a family of their own.

There would be times my reactions become a repetitive cycle of my parents' as I am with my own children. On one occasion, I released my frustration in an inappropriate matter to the point I was back to being that little girl stuck in between my parents. My heart was back to bleeding again but now experiencing the duplicate pain all over again.

I learn a lot from my children at times we may not even realize it. On one occasion, instead of me having a conversation, I was raising my voice until the point they would shut down. I was taking my anger out on them and didn't fully realize it until they voiced their opinion. I had to swallow my pride. I was raised in a household where voices were raised in a conversation but not really grasping the concept of knowing there is a different tone that can be used when having a conversation. It took me what seemed like forever to turn down the tone when having a conversation in order for my children to truly hear the words and not the noise that was coming from my mouth into their ears. Frustrating is an understatement because I was being a part of the breakdown with my own children and didn't know I was unintentionally bleeding their heart as well.

DO I NOT MATTER?

It came to a point I had to accept my part of allowing myself to bleed all out to my children due to me not handling my frustration better being the adult to walk away until things cool down. Or better yet, ignoring the noise just to allow my children to maintain some peace in the presence of both parents. It's not saying you are belittling yourself worth for the other parent's involvement; you are rather taking on the better judgment in fighting your battles. It's unfortunate how many battles we, as parents, have, and losing one battle for a piece of peace is asking for too much to overthink a moment in time. I wished my parents would have picked better battles because all of them are not worth fighting for, only to end up back at square one with no results. Therefore, take a moment to secure your position in your children and trust and believe, when the time comes for questioning, you just will be there to answer.

It was the hardest thing I had to accept, but I knew the effects of a bleeding heart. If you don't correct it, you, too, can become exhausted to the point you can no longer leave an imprint of your love inside their hearts. I had to face my issues and not allow my children to become the target.

Learning to redirect my frustration and how to move past the current situation at hand; repairing my own bleeding heart was my mission to understand my power to heal. This was a test of my strength to move forward in making sure I did my part in knowing that not only do I matter, but my children matter as well.

It took some time, and it still and always will be a work in progress, but at least it's making strides to improve

DO I NOT MATTER?

the situation. Know how to express your feeling without raising an eyebrow or bursting into a sweat. You can have the passion for molding your children but, don't be the person to be overly passionate; you are destroying fragile partials along the way. When I started to make adjustments in my behavior, I noticed the conversation improved. We would be able to sit and have conversations and fill the room with laughter versus the silent cries that went unnoticed.

I, too, would scream out in agonizing pain as I held onto stuff that should have been trashed a long time ago. I carried so much baggage of my past it was tarnishing the relationship with my children. I needed a direction in raising them but didn't have much to turn to. I had to play the role for multiple people, and I am the only one on the team showing up for practice. It became overwhelming to the point the little girl sat in the corner and cried herself to sleep at night to get up and do it all over again the next day.

My heart bled so much at one point I thought it was going to bleed out to the pavement I paced on every day, trying to get it right. Staying alone with my thoughts, which began to run wild, kept me as a loner. Alone to hear the voices of advice, which I know it was God speaking to me, as He was answering my prayers to become a better friend, mother, and self so I don't fake the pain I carried and continue to destroy the love that surrounded me. My children.

Understanding the blood that was shed between the pain of parents, we need to be honest and ask ourselves, "Is it truly worth it?" If not, be okay with returning to the basics of the beginning of your relationship, which started with a conversation. A conversation which now includes a child, but remembers the place of happiness that you both experienced; now, radiate it off to the children to understand that people do change and that hope exists. We just have to get to know one another again, respect the decision, and embrace the future of raising the next generation to evolve beyond our wildest thoughts.

No need to use a band aid to stop the bleeding, use your presence and your time to heal the heart of an open wound!

DO I NOT MATTER?

*Power Of Manifesting Your
Worth = You Matter*

*You
Outstanding
Unique*

*Manifest
Abundance
Transparent
Truth
Enormous
Radiant*

ACKNOWLEDGMENTS

The path you have taken me was necessary. Even when I thought I failed You, You accepted me back. You understand my pain— a pain enough to know what it feels like to become better than my circumstances. Trusting me to surrender to be used for a bigger purpose than expected, but You knew I would be the child who would be strong enough to handle adversity to persevere. I am forever grateful to You, my Lord and Savior, for Your guidance and endless covering through the journey called life.

My Children: You loving me is what I needed to love you harder to do better for us. Even when there was fog blocking out the vision, the sky was always the limit. Making a difference in me was a reward I am honored to pass onto you. To embrace life's journey with your eyes open to know there is a destiny and purpose for you as well. With all my heart, I know you will make me proud, but most importantly, you will make the next chapters of your life a work of art which Picasso is ready to display. Allow God to use you and always put HIM first. Love always and forever, MOM

GG's Babies: Isayah, Claudia-Joy, Bria & BriaVanni - The joy formed on your face when you see me is a direct reflection on the imprint you placed in your heart for me. Know you are powerful, resilient, and valuable to many, but few will truly understand. Walk in your greatness and make the next generation proud because of the possibilities instilled in you. Always keep God first and close. Respect your parents and love on those who love you back. Love always, your GG

Parents: I thank my parents for providing me with the possibility to change. Change to understand it does not reside in my comfort zone.

Family/Friends/Supports: The journey has not been easy, and for you to show you care, I am forever grateful.

ABOUT THE AUTHOR

Vanessa Canteberry is the Founder and CEO of InspiredByVanessa. She was born and raised in Chicago, Illinois. She's determined to continue to break the cycle of poverty, negligent, and unnecessary hardship. Vanessa worked in Corporate America for 20 years as a Secretary. After being laid off in 2011, she knew something needed to change, knowing she was a single parent of three. Vanessa was not able to obtain employment, and the mere thought of being unable to support her son attending high school and two daughters attending college was unbearable.

For that reason, Vanessa challenged herself. She took a stand on faith and changed her mindset. She's on a mission to educating individuals on the importance of transformation of the W2 mindset in life and business.

Now, she is a business owner, Speaker, Mindset Coach, co-host on Motivate Social Podcast, Best Selling Author, working from the comfort of her home. She is also committed to teaching individuals how they, too, can become a business owner and overcome obstacles in their life.

Your past does not determine your destiny; make what seems impossible possible. InspiredByVanessa stands on

FAITH and refuses to allow FEAR to void VISIONS that need to be seen and heard on so many platforms. She teaches you that you are more than a W2.

Vanessa is the Best Selling Author of Shifting Your Mindset and Breaking the Cycle of Brokenness, Co-Author I Am More Than and Do I Not Matter?

You are not alone in your journey!

Feel free to stay connected with Vanessa Canteberry on Social Media at

www.Facebook.com/InspireVanessa

www.Instgram.com/InspiredByVanessa

www.Twitter.com/InspireVanessa

www.Linkedin.com/in/vanessacanteberry

www.InspiredByVanessa.com

www.ingramcontent.com/pod-product-compliance
Lightning Source LLC
Chambersburg PA
CBHW071638040426
42452CB00009B/1684